GW00731439

LOOK BACK,
STRIDE FORWARD

PLEASE RETURN TO:-
WOMENS SUPPORT PROJECT
NEWLANDS CENTRE
871 SPRINGFIELD ROAD
GLASGOW G31 4HQ
041-554 5669

Acknowledgements

We would like to thank Monica, Nicola, Lynne, Judith, Jill, Gary, and the many others who helped to put this book together.

LOOK BACK, STRIDE FORWARD

Miriam Saphira and Lyndy McIntyre

Papers Inc.
P.O. Box 47-398,
Ponsonby,
Auckland,
New Zealand.

First Published in 1989
Papers Inc. PO Box 47-398
Ponsonby, Auckland New Zealand

Cover Design: Lyndy McIntyre
Design: Monica van Tuil
Typsetting: Auckland University Students' Association.
Printing: Interprint, Haltain St, Auckland.

This book is copyright and within the terms of the
Copyright Act no part may be reproduced by any process
without the prior permission of the authors.

Copyright © 1988 Miriam Saphira & Lyndy McIntyre

ISBN 0-908780-06-0

CONTENTS

1
INTRODUCTION
Is this a book for me?

Many of our friends may not be having an easy time, or there may be difficulties in their lives. We hope this book will help you support and understand them. You may also have had a hard time and you may find this information useful for your own understanding and healing.

Many of us have received abuse as children and young people. The abuse may be verbal, physical, sexual, emotional, or neglectful and it may not affect us until we are older.

Sometimes we do not consider the hidings that we got, or the degrading nicknames, such as, Fatty, Clumsy Carol, Smartypants, Lazybones, as abuse. We may not connect the abuse to the way we feel about ourselves now. This may be the reason that we do not feel very good about ourselves no matter how hard we try or how much we achieve.

2
DEFINITIONS

Physical abuse is hitting, punching, whipping, pinching, pushing, scratching or shaking of a young person by an adult or a person who may be older and bigger.

Sexual abuse occurs when a child is used sexually by an adult or a person, three or more years older. They may do this through unfair influence, exploitation and threats. Sexual abuse may include touching, exposure of an erect penis, coaxing the child to touch the adult, oral sex, finger penetration or rape.

Emotional abuse is the use of threats, persuasion, bossing or an adult taking advantage of a young person to gain power over you. It can also involve putdowns and negative statements regarding a young person's worth.

NEGLECT IS ALSO ABUSE

Physical Neglect is the lack of food, warmth, or clothing.

Emotional Neglect is the lack of love, hugging and positive statements regarding a young person's value.

Sexual Neglect is when an adult denies a young person's sexual right to masturbate or express themselves sexually among their peers.

BIG HURTS AND LITTLE HURTS

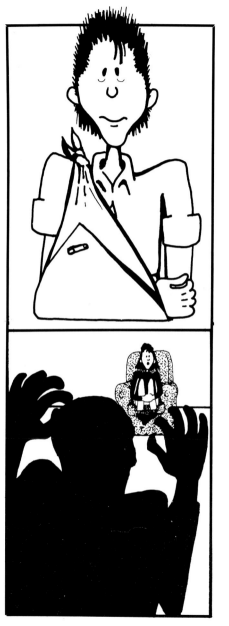

We have all experienced hurts during our childhood. Some of these experiences have helped us to adjust to the real world. After all, our parents are human, they make mistakes from time to time. However, some of the hurts can go deeper. Some of the mistakes made by our parents were very big mistakes. It is difficult for these deep hurts to heal. Sometimes unhealed hurts make us do things in a particular way. This can become a pattern.

9

3
DEFENCES

We may react with defences. This is the way we block off what is happening to us to protect ourselves. There are a number of ways we can do this.

LIGHTENING THE LOAD

We may play down hurtful experiences.   "It wasn't anything."

All abuse is important to an individual person. It is not what actually occurred that is so important to us but what impact it had on our feelings, and our lives. When it was happening to us we sometimes suffered with fear and distress for days and weeks.

EXPLANATION

We may explain what was done to us by finding a reason for the other person's behaviour.

"My mum was having a hard time."

"My dad loved me but he just got it all wrong."

"My parents just didn't know what was the right thing to do for us kids."

Many of our parents are not informed and have difficulties but they also have a responsibility to care for us in the best possible way. We cannot carry their responsibilities on our shoulders. That is their job.

It is also their responsibility to seek help for their problems.

FORGETTING SOME OF IT

We may not be able to remember very much of the abuse. At times it seems as if we have forgotten some of the worst bits. We will need a lot of support and caring if we are to begin to unravel all of those horrible situations in our past.

"It's too awful to remember."

"It's all in the past. I just want to forget."

We try to forget the past. In doing so, we may develop certain ways to help us to cope with the abuse.

CUTTING OFF OUR FEELINGS

Defences cut off our feelings.
This may be a way for us to cope with a situation that is happening but if it becomes a pattern we will be stuck and this is not constructive for us.

"I feel numb."

"I'm tough, I can cope."

"I can't talk about it. The words won't come."

WE MUST FIND SOMEONE THAT WE CAN TALK TO

We can talk to our best friend, to grandma, to auntie, to a social worker or counsellor or to brothers and sisters or anyone we feel we can trust or that we know well. We do need to talk.

4
WAYS OF FEELING

There are many different ways of feeling when we have been abused or neglected in some way. Here are some of the feelings that were expressed in the first Incest Survivors' Group report in New Zealand. Several other young people who have had very difficult childhoods have also contributed to this section.

FEELING RESPONSIBLE

"I feel responsible. Keeping a secret was a very heavy burden. I learned to keep my mouth closed and now I find it difficult to talk openly. Even when I was talking about everyday things I was frightened that terrible words would tumble out of my mouth. I learned to say a lot less. I have become quiet and even secretive about many other things too."

"I feel responsible for keeping the family together. If I had told Mum what Dad was doing to me then he would have gone to jail and they would have got a divorce. I didn't want to break up our family, did I?"

FEELING TRICKED.

"I felt tricked into something that I did not understand."

"My innocence was used. I was made to do something I did not want to do. And they called it love. They used to say to me:' You love me don't you?' But they had all the control, and I had none, and they used force to take the control. I learned that if I did everything for them and nothing for me it was called loving them."

FEELING FRIGHTENED

"I was afraid of the dark".
"I was afraid of strangers. I became very shy to protect myself."
"I was afraid of my mother leaving or dying."
"I was afraid of open spaces where there was nowhere to hide."
"I was afraid of crowds and groups of people."

"I was afraid of being alone with a person in what should have been a natural position two people in a room — but knowing all the time that something nasty might happen."

"I was afraid of knowing that the person might visit and I would have to think of a way to get out of seeing them, or being with them, or going anywhere with them."

"I was afraid of games — that they would go on longer than they should and become something else."

"I was frightened to go to sleep because of the terrible dreams I would have."

"I was frightened in my bed."

FEELING DIFFERENT

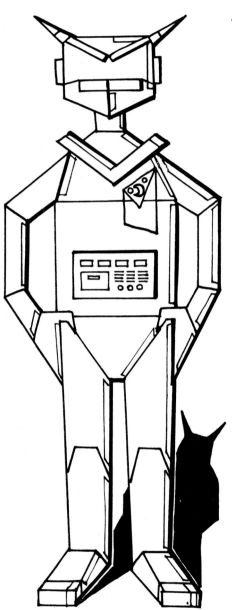

"I felt different from everyone else. I thought everyone could see the difference and they would stare at me."

"I felt lost and alien. I felt divorced from my family."

"When I was asked to say something in class everybody would gawk at me. I felt everybody could see how different I was."

FEELING LONELY

'I felt alone. I could not talk to anyone about it. I battled with myself because I wanted to talk about it but who would have believed me?"

'My family seemed so different from everybody else and I was always by myself. No-one would want to be with me when they found out what my family was like. I felt that I could not talk to the others in my class or they would see how things really were."

FEELING OLD

"I felt old because I felt so responsible for everyone being happy. If they weren't happy I felt responsible to make them happy."

"I felt distanced from other children and distanced from other people. Being in league with an adult instead of being protected by him made me feel responsible for him, and responsible for keeping his secret."

FEELING GUILTY

"I thought it was my fault. I thought I had done something to make it happen, that everyone must know what had happened and know that it was my fault."

FEELING ASHAMED

"I felt ashamed. I felt that I was dirty and bad for what had happened."

"I felt that if I had been good it would not have happened. I felt ashamed that I had been belted."

FEELING BEWILDERED

"I did not understand what was happening. The sense of bewilderment stayed for a long time."

"I felt confused. I did not know anything about sex so I did not understand what was happening to me. It was a real puzzle. No matter how hard I tried, I was wrong. I felt puzzled that everything was so unfair."

FEELING INSECURE

"I felt insecure and anxious. I did not want to leave home and yet home was where the bad things happened. I hung around Mum and it only made her madder with me."

"Even when I tried real hard, things seemed to go wrong. It didn't seem to matter what I was doing, they would still yell and hit me."

FEELING VULNERABLE

"I felt vulnerable. When the teacher made sexual innuendos, I thought they were directed to me. I was particularly aware of and could recognise a sexual advance or approach from miles away."

FEELING
SEPARATED

"I felt separated from my friends. I felt separated from myself. It was as if I was in separate pieces with different things happening to me and happening all at the same time."

FEELING SICK

"When I thought about what had happened I felt sick — squeasy, yukky, squirmy sicky feelings."

"When I had to stand for a long time I wanted to vomit."

"When he ejaculated in my mouth I vomited."

HOW DO I FEEL ABOUT THE PERSON WHO ABUSED ME?

"My feelings change a lot. I really like my big brother, but I don't like what he did. When things were bad with our parents he looked after me and protected me from all the fights."

"I really hate my Dad. I hate what he did to me and Mum. I never want to see him again."

"I feel really sad about my Mum. She never enjoyed us. She was so full of anger. Always hitting us. I sort of love her but I don't want to see her."

"I feel so angry. I shout and yell a lot. I am angry at Mum for not protecting me like a mother should. I am angry at my father for doing what hé did. I am angry at the police. I am angry at the social workers. They make me sick."

"I feel that I have to look after everyone. That I am to blame in some way and have to make everything all right. There must be some reason for it all. I guess I feel angry because I could not stop it all. I am frustrated that I had no control, and everyone else has all the power."

A FEELING SCALE.

We can make ourselves a scale to see how we feel about particular people each day or every week. We will often find that our feelings change with time.

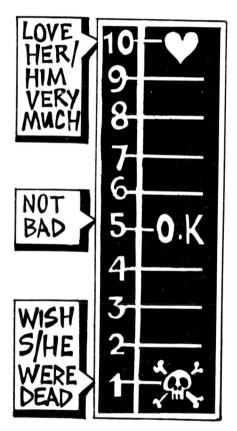

HOW DO I FEEL
ABOUT MY MOTHER?

Our mothers may have found the situation too difficult for them to deal with. Sometimes they could not see what was happening because they felt they did not have the strength to handle it. Some of our mothers are jealous of us. They feel things are easier than it was for their generation. Some mothers are so insecure that they worry about losing their financial security, marriage or social status and they feel that they have to put that before our needs and our rights.

These feelings do not make it all right that abuse has happened. It is our mother's responsiblity to get help and stop the abuse.

As one of the members of the first Christchurch Incest Survivors' Group said about her relationship with her mother:
" I felt I had to protect her from knowledge as she wouldn't have been able to handle it and she has enough worries anyway.
"I did not feel angry towards her, as she often protected me from my father's physical violence or emotional unpleasantness. Sometimes she got beaten up instead of me. I felt a sense of guilt towards her because she had protected me in other ways. I felt she was as powerless as I was to stop the abuse. I felt angry with her for protecting my father's memory. I could never allow her to feel tenderness or grief towards my father's memory as I could not feel those things, only anger. My mother has cut off from me to protect the family. It distanced me from my mother, the only parent I felt I really had and desperately wanted to be close to. It totally disturbed my relationship with my mother. It is only since talking to her about the group and discovering that she was molested as a child that things have been better."

We have many different feelings towards our mothers.

"I feel angry towards my Mum. She never stood up for us. She never stopped the hidings and the sex. She was the Mother; she should have been able to do something about it."

"I love my Mum. I never want her to find out. I do not want anything to happen that will hurt her."

"Now I feel alone. I cannot feel close to anybody in my family."

"I feel distanced from my mother. I feel different. I think that people are always staring at me or that they know all about what happened to me. No matter what clothes I wear or how many times I wash myself I feel that people can see it. I feel marked."

"I feel that I don't even have a Mum."

"I wish I could go out and buy a new Mum. I just can't get on with that woman who says she is my mother."

5
DIFFICULTIES

MY FEELINGS HAVE LED TO SOME DIFFICULTIES

"Now I cannot trust people."

Eliana Gil in her book "Outgrowing The Pain" says this about trust:
"Trust is a major issue for all people, and especially for adults abused as children. They have difficulty trusting their own reactions, thoughts, feelings, and perceptions."

Trust is an important part of human relationships. When we feel unable to trust people we have difficulty finding and keeping friends. The less we trust, the less likely we are to make friends or have close relationships. The fewer friends we have, the worse we feel about ourselves. The more isolated we become, the less we can trust others. When others do not seek us out, or we cannot seem to make friends, we may think that there is something wrong with ourselves. Then we

can feel vulnerable, and need protection, so we often guard ourselves and do not have enough trust to be open.

When we were children we trusted that our parents would feed us, change our nappies and keep us safe and warm. If this did not happen our trust was broken and now it is difficult to restore.

Our parents may not have been very consistent. Sometimes when we cried they comforted us and at other times they may have hit us for crying. So we learned not to expect much from others. To change this we may have to take small risks with trustworthy people. This happens bit by bit. We may think that no-one, is trustworthy so we may sabotage our friends attempts to comfort us.

"You say you know how I feel. No-one can know how I feel. Leave me alone."

When I say that to my friends when they are trying to help me I may be actually saying that I think that I am not worth their care or affection because I feel bad about myself.

DIFFICULTIES
WITH SELF ESTEEM

"I must have been bad or my parents would have loved me and looked after me."

"My Mum hit me when I was naughty. I got hit a lot so I must be a very bad person."

Many of us heard our parents say how bad we were. When we made a mistake we might have got lots of feedback. We may have been told how bad we were. We may not have got the praise we deserved when we did something right. Yet it is hard for us to criticise our parents because we are so dependent on them. We still want and need their love and if we say that our parents are bad then we feel that they will certainly not love us. When we have been abused we tend to divide the world in two parts, either good or bad. If I am all bad then I may see my parents as all good. Sometimes I will think that every-one is out to get me and I probably deserve it. But I get afraid of people and afraid of being hurt.

DIFFICULTIES WITH PROTECTING MYSELF

"Sometimes I protected myself by being especially good and working very hard. I did not make friends and studied a great deal."

"I protected myself by joining a gang. I felt powerful and safe when there was a lot of us together."

"I protected myself by eating. I ate so much that I became very fat and nobody wanted to be my friend so I felt bad all over again."

"If I keep myself away from other people then they will not tell me that I am bad or abuse me."

"If I expect nothing then I will not be disappointed, so I will never ask for anything. Or I may ask for impossible things to make sure that I will get nothing because that is what I deserve. This will keep my self concept in one piece. If I am a bad person I will remain a bad person."

DIFFICULTIES WITH LOVING MYSELF.

Sometimes we feel that we are bad and that we are not worthy of being loved. We feel unable to take care of and nurture ourselves. We may work very hard and not take time to enjoy ourselves. We may feel it is not worth the effort to do anything for ourselves so we do not change our clothes as often as we should. We may neglect to take a bath, to shave, to change our tampon/sanitary pad regularly. We may not eat the right foods so our skin becomes spotty and we just say that we do not care what we look like.

DIFFICULTIES WITH ATTAINMENT

At school or work we may feel that we have to work harder than anyone else because we are not as

good as other people. No matter how much we accomplish we still do not overcome these feelings so we drive ourselves on and on and on. For others it may be the opposite.

"I am so useless at everything, what is the point of trying? If I do not try then I cannot fail."

We may be frightened of being successful because people will notice us. We may feel uncomfortable when people praise us.

It may be helpful to think about, and even write down, what things we like to do and what things we like to get praised for. Are there situations where we can enjoy praise? We may want to ask our friends why praise makes us feel uncomfortable.

DIFFICULTIES MAKING FRIENDS

We can act in extreme ways by making a friend and clinging to them so they become suffocated by us. We may telephone them several times a day. We are always thinking of reasons to drop in on them. When they are too busy to attend to our demands we feel they have rejected us.

We may be so tense and anxious in social situations that other people get an idea that they make us uncomfortable so they keep away from us. This makes us feel that no-one likes us so we are always feeling like an intruder.

We may be so busy protecting ourselves that we do not let people close to us because of our tough image. We may do this by being gruff or not talking very much.

If this is happening to you there may be ways you can change it. A counsellor may help you to overcome feeling uncomfortable in social situations. We can check that we are not telephoning and visiting our friends too frequently. If we think this is happening we may be able to visit and telephone several different aquaintances. Talking to our friends at school and work may help us find out what type of friendship they would like to have with us.

1.

2.

3.

4.

6
OUR PLACE IN THE WORLD

WE HAVE DEVELOPED PATTERNS OF RELATING TO THE WORLD

We learn to act in certain ways when we are young. We can get stuck in these patterns as we grow up. The patterns can change how we see things and how we relate to other people.

I AM A CARETAKER

"I like to look after other people and take care of them. I love to give to others that is why I became a masseuse /social worker/ waitress/teacher/nurse/babysitter."

If we look after other people we will always be needed. We become very good at giving but find receiving difficult. Sometimes in this role we encourage dependency yet we begin to resent those who rely on us.

"If I work like this I must have a balance to ensure that I do not become resentful. I must have a balance and learn to like receiving things too."

I AM SEXUALLY AVAILABLE

"I have sex a lot. It makes me feel needed and wanted. I can get affection from the person for that moment and leading up to the sex bit I feel useful. I feel unable to refuse when some one makes a pass at me. It is as if my role in life is to have sex and keep other people happy. I guess I am a sexual caretaker."

Sex can be used to express affection and to make a baby but it can also be used to release tension, to pursue pleasure, to create bonds, to prove to ourselves how popular we are, to rebel against our family, to sell things, to earn money or goods, to pay back a debt, to gain power over another person, to oppress,

or to prove our identity. Some of these ways of using sex do not have a good effect on us. We put ourselves down. Masturbation, jogging, swimming and deep breathing are other ways of releasing tension and learning about ourselves.

There may be other ways to gain popularity other than having sex with someone.

I AM A HIDER

"I am hidden away. I try very hard not to be noticed. I like my hair to fall over my face so that I cannot see people and they cannot see me. Best of all I like staying in my room."

We have many ways that we can hide from the outside world even when we have to go out in it.

We can wear lots of clothes or heavy coats. We can eat a lot and hide in the fat or we can diet so much that we become slim enough not to be noticed. We might not like to wear bright colours or fashion clothes in case someone should notice us.

As well as recognising the way we do things it can be a good idea to talk to others about how we feel.

I AM REAL TOUGH

"I am so tough nothing hurts me. I don't let anyone too close to me and I never cry. If I think I might have a tear I clap someone on the back, make a loud noise, go to the toilet or get a drink. I like to drink a lot and even tell others about how much I drank or how out of it I got last night."

We can toughen our image in many ways. Sometimes our tension and anger frightens other people away. Sometimes we may use drugs or alcohol to lessen the pain and make us feel numb.

"I liked to drink until my face felt numb and everything became hazy or I would go to bed and hide in my bed, even taking sleeping pills so I could stay asleep longer. I didn't realise that I was missing out on all the good things in life as well."

I AM SICK

"I can't take any more. Please look after me. My head aches and when that is better I get a cold or my stomach gets upset. I really want to be looked after. I want to be relieved from all the responsibilities that I have been carrying."

We may have lots of accidents. Sometimes we are too preoccupied with our troubles to take care. Other times we just do not look after ourselves. We must remember that we only have one body and we need to look after it so that we can live our lives more easily.

I WISH I WERE DEAD

"I don't know why I was born. I don't want to be here any more. I wish I were dead. Nobody understands what it is like."

When we feel unable to lessen our pain we may start seeing suicide as a way out. We may start reading about death, taking an interest in the different ways that people die. This may lead to us hurting ourselves. Sometimes we cut or burn ourselves to tell people the way we are feeling and that we need some help. Sometimes the sharp objects we dig into ourselves are a way of punishing ourselves.

It may also reassure us that we are still alive and still have feelings like other people. Talking about the way we feel to a close friend can be helpful. Some people find keeping a diary or journal and writing how we feel about events and things around us is helpful.

47

I AM GOING TO EXPLODE

"I feel so angry I am going to explode. If he wants to look at me like that I'll give him something to think about."

When we feel like this we are always looking for a fight. We fly off the handle with the slightest provocation. We are always ready to do battle and sometimes join causes just because we can identify with their sense of outrage.

7
MAKING CHANGES

CHANGING TO LET GO
OF OUR PAST

It is easy for us to resent our childhood. Sometimes we tell other people how unfair everything is and we resent people who have got a better life than we think we have. There are several things we can do to allow us to see good things around us. We can love ourselves, change our patterns, get rid of our guilty feelings, plan ahead, see a counsellor about our anger, get involved in outside activities, take up a new interest, join a club, or do some healing exercises.

LOVING YOURSELF

You are a worthwhile person and deserve to grow and change. You deserve and have a right to happiness. Have you ever thought of yourself as a survivor?

"I have survived a difficult childhood. Things have not been easy and yet I am able to get up in the morning and get dressed and I get to work and to school. This makes me a strong person."

"I am a worthwhile person and I deserve some good things. I deserve my own love."

IT'S NOT EASY TO CHANGE

We can always think of excuses why we do not need to change what we usually do. What we know and are familar with is usually the most comfortable. It is the safest way for us that we have learned. It feels very risky and unsafe to try to do things a new way.

"I found practising something before I tried it was useful. I used to make up conversations to practise. When I first tried going out I always went with a friend then I could talk about how I was feeling. That was very helpful."

By keeping things the same we are trying to protect ourselves. What are we protecting ourselves from? How can we protect ourselves in a different way so that we can change and grow?

SPRING CLEANING

We need to get rid of our feelings of guilt and responsiblity in order to love ourselves. One way of doing this is when we are in the shower we can think about the ways we feel responsible. Allow those feelings to merge into the running water and then wash off us and down the plug hole. We can start from the top of our head as we rub the shampoo into our hair and let the feelings of guilt and responsibility run down our body and off.

We can do the same when we are taking a bath. By just closing our eyes we can imagine those feelings as a colour and then they colour the water and then the water becomes clear again as the colour evaporates with the steam. After our bath or shower we can massage our body with our hand and some lotion or oil, Using long caressing strokes we can say to ourselves that we deserve these good feelings. "I love me. I love me." It is important to love yourself.

PLANNING

aunt could never understand why I couldn't save money to visit her and why I couldn't think to be prepared. I never could even remember to have a supply of tampons or hair clips to pin my hair up for gym. It's been a hard struggle to learn how to save and make plans."

If we expect others to hurt us, disappoint us or dislike us, we may find it difficult to think ahead.

Sometimes we can plan some things such as our homework or swotting but we cannot manage to plan the things that are more home based. A useful way to change is to keep a diary or calendar and plan the next week. We can plan our wardrobe and cut out pictures from magazines of the fashions that we like and write up how much they will cost. Then we can save towards them. We might plan how we could rearrange our room.

Why is planning ahead so difficult?

"I learned not to plan things, so that I would not be disappointed when they didn't happen."

"I could never think ahead. To do that would remind me that HE might abuse me again. My

HEALING OUR INNER CHILD

When we have been hurt as a child we can no longer meet life with playfulness and love. We have lost the delight in testing our strength and limitations as we explore the world. We need to stop searching for the parents that we never had. We can nurture ourselves by our daily breathing. Each time we take a breath we can think of our favourite colour. We can allow ourselves to feel the warmth of that colour spreading through us and as we breathe out we can let any tension, pain, anger or blame be released from us. When we are day dreaming it can be very healing to try to visualise an alternative childhood from the one that we had. Then we can acknowledge the painful experiences. The focus should be on our view of what happened and it how it affected us. The focus should not be on **why** it happened.

NURTURING OURSELVES

There are many ways that we can nurture ourselves but they may not all be good for us. Feeding ourselves is one way we nurture ourselves but if we fill ourselves up with chocolate fish like I have just eaten, then we are likely to get pimples and end up feeling bad about ourselves. If we write a list of all the food, drinks, activities, clothes, music, books, pictures on our wall and the company of friends we enjoy, on bad days we can look down our list and see what we can treat ourselves with. We can also put down how often we can enjoy something before it is too much for us. Some things like affection we may never feel we can get enough of.

Mae West said "Too much of a good thing is wonderful" .

Here is a list of the things that I enjoy:

Rock melons and grapes
Walking   Licorise allsorts
Snowfreeze   Breakfast in bed
Fashion   Listening to music .
Singing   money   Science fiction
Writing   Playing my guitar
Massage   Getting Letters
Cooking   Bubble baths   Parties
Sketching   Riding a motor bike
Skating   Brushing my hair
movies   wearing a silk shirt
Swimming   thriller   Chocolate fish
Reading a   Travelling in a train
Shopping   Being with my friends
Kissing   Space invaders
Sport   A big mac

MAKING JUDGEMENTS

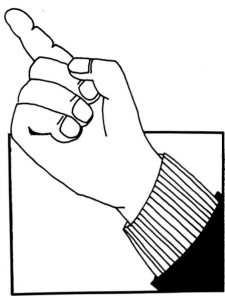

If we are making judgements about other people we are probably repeating the judgements that were made about us as children. If we listen to the words and the tone of voice that we use, we may remember when we had that very thing said to us. Just imagine yourself as a judge. What sort of picture do you see yourself as? Are you a force of nature, a killer, a stern authoritarian figure, a teacher, an alien, or a dominating person? Sometimes the harshest judge is the judgement that we use on ourselves. As we breathe in we can affirm ourselves with the knowledge that we are a good person.

"I am a good person."

"I have many talents."

"Sometimes I may make mistakes

but I forgive myself. Everybody makes mistakes."
"I am a worthwhile person".
"I am a loving, caring person." How many more positive statements can we make about ourselves?

When we make gross negative statements we can make them more positive by rephrasing them. The statement: "I am always breaking things" can be changed to: "Today I broke two plates when I was washing up but last week I washed the dishes without breaking a thing."

HEALING THROUGH TALKING

Forming a group to talk about our lives and our childhood experiences has helped many of us to change tha patterns that we developed as children. The group has helped us deal with the things we had no power to change. Some of us have found it easier to talk to a close friend or a counsellor while others of us have found a small group better to start with.

More schools are setting up groups for young people who have something in common whether it is sexual abuse, parents divorcing, parents are homosexual or belong to another minority group, a father in prison or parents who are alcoholic. A group helps us overcome the feeling that "I am the only one in the world who has had this experience." Some young people have organised their own groups because they feel that adults already have too much control over the things they want to do.

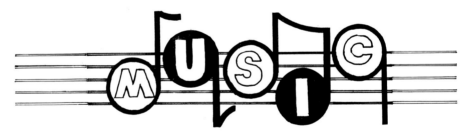

HEALING THROUGH MUSIC

One way we can explore the different ways that we feel is through listening to music. Different types of music can set our mood, laughing, lilting, light music as opposed to authoritarian marching music.
" I like flute music when I want to feel relaxed. When I am studying I like listening to the lastest hits."

By selecting our music we can change the way we are currently feeling to gain control over our moods.

HEALING THROUGH DRAWING

By taking our favourite pencil, pastel or crayon we can allow ourselves the freedom of moving it in broad strokes over the page. This can be very good when it is done in a small group and when we feel we have finished we can talk about what we have created or we may be quite happy just to have done it and not share it with others. We do not have to have the skills of Picasso or Van Gogh to make it a very healing action. We can ask ourselves what colour have we used? Why did we choose that particular colour? We can draw different things. We can draw how we saw our family when we were five years old, nine years old, or eleven years old, and we can draw the family we wish we had.

"One day some of us drew a picture of our mothers and ourselves. It was so interesting. Some mothers were smaller than their daughters or sons, others were very big and some did not have faces. Some were holding hands and touching while others were distant and some were protecting each other."

If we are feeling brave we can draw things that we are frighten-ed of.
We can draw our dreams and our wishes.

HEALING THROUGH WRITING

Writing our feelings each day into a journal can be very helpful. Some people have found writing out their bad experiences has ended up as a book. Iris Galey, who wrote "I Couldn't Cry When Daddy Died", found it a very good way to recover from incest. Other books are "Searching For Spring" by Patricia Murphy and "Cry Hard and Swim" by Jacqueline Spring. Some people like to get a friend or counsellor to read what they have written. Others like to keep it to themselves.

ANGER

What makes us angry? We can certainly feel angry about the abuse we received but we often feel really angry in other situations now. We may need to stop ourselves reacting furiously and think about the situation. What is making us feel so powerless? What can we do to change that?

We may need to work out ways of ridding ourselves of our angry feelings. We can talk about it, do some physical activity like running, swimming, chopping wood, punching pillows, taking a shower, having a hot bath, or giving ourselves a foot or neck massage. Have you tried any of these things?

"Some days I wake up and seem to have a day of angry feelings. When I try to talk about how this or that really pisses me off, I find that I am really feeling angry at something else. Then I find it useful to think what I can do to change things. Most of my anger is about things that I can't change. I get really angry when I do not have control over parts of my life. A friend taught me to write down all the areas of my life where I **have** got some control and see how I could organise those things better. When it is past things, I still find it difficult to let go of that anger and look at my future. But I am changing all that slowly."

"I was so frightened of my anger. A friend had been to a counsellor so we started talking about being angry. We tried saying what we thought would happen if we let ourselves get angry. We were so similar except she was the one labelled bad-tempered. I was referred to as 'difficult'. Well, we changed that. We started to have regular 'talk' times and I found it so useful that I got involved in starting a support group at school. I still have a few bad days but there's heaps of good ones too."

NOTHING MATTERS ANY MORE

"Sometimes I turn my anger on myself and feel what's the use? Nothing matters. As soon as I started to talk to someone about feeling this way I found that things did seem to matter a bit more. I wanted my friend to be happy and not to hear all my complaints so I had to think of something positive, even though at the time it was difficult."

It is important to find someone to talk to if we are feeling depressed. If we draw a chart of our childhood and mark in some of the bad things we can also mark in the good things we can remember, even circling them with a red pen can sometimes help us realise that bright patches do occur in our lives.

HEALING THROUGH OUR BODIES

We can read our bodies and see how we relate to the outside world.

"If my shoulders droop and I hang my head I am hiding away from everybody. So I throw my head back and straighten my shoulders. It is very hard to do. I am so used to hiding that this new way is very uncomfortable. Maybe it is because I feel ashamed of myself. The reasons are not so important now. Being free to be the real me is what is important to me. Now I am going to practise every morning so that I can hold my head as high as anyone."

Our bodies are very useful to get rid of tensions and negative thoughts. We can dance and sing and lift up our spirits. We can do

this for ourselves whenever we wish to.

"I'm real moody and I know my friends find it difficult. Then I thought I am bloody lucky to have friends who put up with my moods so I began to do something about it. When I feel a bit shitty I stamp when I walk and say to myself 'No! No! "I was amazed the first time, cos the real reason I felt moody just popped into my head. I was so full of resentment — even towards my own friends. It doesn't happen every time but after a few hard stamps, I usually feel in a better mood."

"I find that my body is so useful. I can give it long baths or massage my feet and rub oils into my legs and I always feel better about myself. I even did a project at school about body language and watched a video. I got good marks but most of all I learned how to see myself and how I am feeling by the way that I stand and sit. I feel that I am getting better every day."

BUILDING ON OUR TALENTS.

You say that you haven't got any? It is so much easier to think of the things that we are not so good at. This fits with our concept of ourselves as a bad person. We may have become very good at some of the 'bad' things we do so we have developed some strengths after all. Now we can learn to relocate our strengths.

"I could never concentrate at school so my work is never very good as I am really so far behind. Then I realised that I do very neat headings so I can do good work in the way it is set out."

"I work at the supermarket every night and I am always on time. I did not realise that I am very good at keeping time."

WILL I ABUSE MY PETS? LATER, WILL I ABUSE MY CHILDREN?

We often read that parents who abuse their children had a difficult childhood. This may make us worry that we will be a bad parent. We may find ourselves pulling the cat's tail. We may call our pets nasty names when we are in a bad mood. This may spread to other animals or to our brothers and sisters. Getting to know how we feel and expressing the feelings in ways that do not hurt anybody will be important. We will have to recognise those hidden feelings of revenge and anger.

"I thought it would be smart to shut the cat in the cupboard all day and then I forgot her. Now I am beginning to understand what I was really thinking then."

"I just wanted to punch him when I thought he had it so good. I never stopped to think that he may not be having an easy time either."

"I felt like pinching my younger sister. Sometimes I used to do that. I wanted to see her hurt like I was hurting. Now I have learned to talk about my feelings and I find I do not feel that I have to act on them."

"I used to like seeing other kids crying. It took me quite a while to work out that it was because I could not cry. So I stopped saying spiteful things to upset other people. I guess it also had a bit of getting my own back too."

It was horrible for us when we were abused so it is important that we do not make a pet or another person miserable because we are hurting. We will need to talk to some one about our feelings so that they do not get distorted.

It was not the cat's fault.

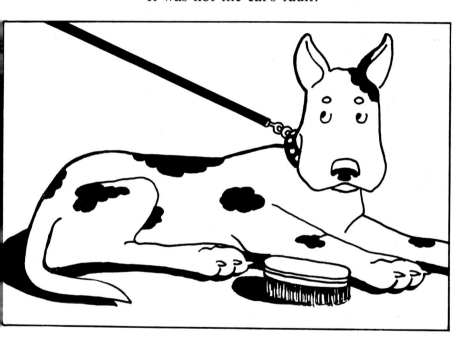

WHO AM I?

Tony was molested by a man and he is worried that because he got an erection he might be homosexual. Tony will only be gay if his identity is already developing in that direction. Sexual abuse does not change our sexual orientation. Tony may want to talk to a counsellor to explore these worries. If a young man thinks he is gay he will find it helpful to get in touch with other young gay men to talk about these new feelings and how this may affect his relationship with his parents. There are support groups in the bigger cities that you can write to.

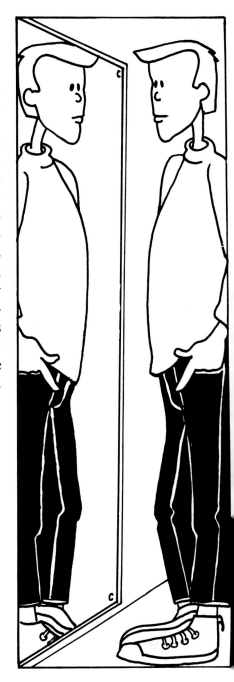

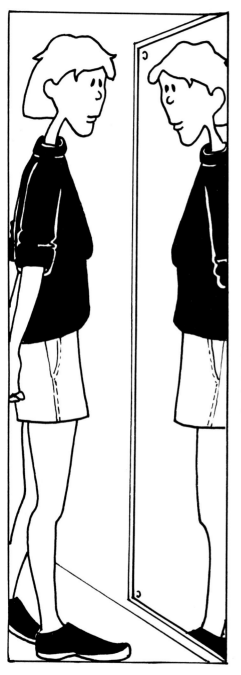

Debby is worried that she might become a lesbian because she is frightened of men. Debby may not develop a sexual relationship until her fears have begun to fade. Strong fear will not change her basic orientation but may make her heterosexual orientation more difficult.

Our basic identity will stay the same even though we now have fears and anxious experiences to deal with. We will handle them with the characteristics that we were born with and have developed through our early childhood. They are the strengths that will help us love ourselves and stride towards choosing those things that we really want to do for ourselves.

COLOURING OURSELVES

Visualize a beautiful colour. Imagine this colour is the colour of the air surrounding you. Breathe deeply and draw this clear, vivid, colourful light into your body. Feel the healing power of this light. Feel its healing vibration as it spreads throughout your body. Feel every cell of your body being coloured with this healing shade. As you breathe out, release any pain or tension you have noticed in your body. Continue to breathe deeply and fill your body with this healing light and release your hurt and pain as you breathe out.

A DIFFICULT TASK

Healing ourselves is a very difficult job. Sometimes we may need to ask for some help from our friends or a counsellor. As well as difficult, healing is also very important so we can enjoy the rest of our lives.

"I'm throwing my shoulders back and starting right now."

WORRIES

So we have read this little book and looked at the pictures. So what. It didn't answer all my questions. Well I guess I can take some responsibility for those questions. If I want to I can ring somebody up. I don't have to give my name. I don't even need to say that I need to know. I'm asking for a friend maybe, after all, I am my best friend. Some of these places may be able to answer those questions:

Rape Crisis   Family Support
Help Foundation   Parent Line
Life Line   Youth Line

Other publications by Papers Inc. include:

Papers Inc.
P.O. Box 47-398,
Ponsonby,
Auckland,
New Zealand.

KATIE'S YUKKY PROBLEM
by Lynda Morgan.
For 4-10 year olds.

DANIEL AND HIS THERAPIST
by Lynda Morgan.
For 5-14 year olds.

MEGAN'S SECRET
by Lynda Morgan.
For 8-16 year olds.

THE SEXUAL ABUSE OF CHILDREN
by Miriam Saphira
An introduction to sexual abuse.